WORLD BELIEFS AND CULTURES

Islam

Revised and updated

Sue Penney

Heinemann
LIBRARY

www.heinemann.co.uk/library
Visit our website to find out more information about Heinemann Library books.

To order:
☎ Phone 44 (0) 1865 888066
🖹 Send a fax to 44 (0) 1865 314091
💻 Visit the Heinemann Bookshop at www.heinemann.co.uk/library to browse our catalogue and order online.

First published in Great Britain by Heinemann Library, Halley Court, Jordan Hill, Oxford OX2 8EJ, part of Pearson Education. Heinemann is a registered trademark of Pearson Education Ltd.

Editorial: Nancy Dickmann
Design: Steve Mead and Debbie Oatley
Picture research: Melissa Allison
Production: Alison Parsons

Originated by Modern Age Repro
Printed and bound in China by Leo Paper Group

13 digit ISBN: 978 0 431 11028 8 (HB)
12 11 10 09 08
10 9 8 7 6 5 4 3 2 1

13 digit ISBN: 978 0 431 11035 6 (PB)
13 12 11 10 09
10 9 8 7 6 5 4 3 2 1

British Library Cataloguing in Publication Data
Penney, Sue
Islam. – (World Beliefs and Cultures)
1. Islam – Juvenile literature
I. Title
297

A full catalogue record for this book is available from the British Library.

Acknowledgements
The publishers would like to thank the following for permission to reproduce copyright material: *Roman transliteration of the Holy Qur'an* with English translation, Abdullah Yusuf Ali, Sh Muhammad Ashraf Publishers, Pakistan.

The publishers would like to thank the following for permission to reproduce photographs: Alamy/Sally and Richard Greenhill p. **18**; Ancient Art and Architecture p. **35**; Andes Press Agency/Carlos Reyes-Manzo p. **40**; Circa Photo Library/William Holtby pp. **25, 31, 32, 41**; PA Photos/AP/Nader Daoud p. **38**; Panos Pictures/Warrick Page p. **37**; Peter Sanders pp. **5, 6, 7, 8, 11, 12, 13, 14, 15, 16, 17, 20, 21, 22, 23, 24, 26, 27, 28, 29, 30, 33, 34, 36, 39**; Photoedit, Inc. pp. **4** (Jeff Greenberg), **19** (A. Ramey), **42** (Bob Daemmrich). Background image on cover and inside book from istockphoto.com/Bart Broek.

Cover photo of Muslims gathering for prayer at the Jama Masjid Mosque, Delhi, reproduced with permission of Alamy/Fredrik Renander.

Our thanks to Philip Emmett for his comments in the preparation of this book.

Every effort has been made to contact copyright holders of any material reproduced in this book. Any omissions will be rectified in subsequent printings if notice is given to the publishers.

Contents

Introducing Islam 4

The life of Muhammad 6

The history of Islam 10

The Qur'an 14

Ways of worship 18

Mosques 22

Hajj – pilgrimage to Makkah 28

Celebrations 30

Family occasions 36

What it means to be a Muslim 42

Map 44

Timeline 45

Glossary 46

Further information 48

Index 48

Any words shown in bold, **like this**, are explained in the glossary.

Dates: In this book, dates are followed by the letters BCE (Before the Common Era) or CE (Common Era). This is instead of using BC (Before Christ) and AD (*Anno Domini* meaning in the year of our Lord). The date numbers are the same in both systems.

Introducing Islam

Islam is the religion of people called Muslims. The word Islam and the word Muslim both come from an **Arabic** word which is best translated as 'submission'. Submission means 'to place under' – in other words, to accept that someone else is more important than yourself, and to obey them. Muslims believe that they submit to **Allah**. Allah is the Arabic word for 'God'. This submission is not like being a slave, obeying without question and with no involvement. It is an active decision to live their lives as Allah wants.

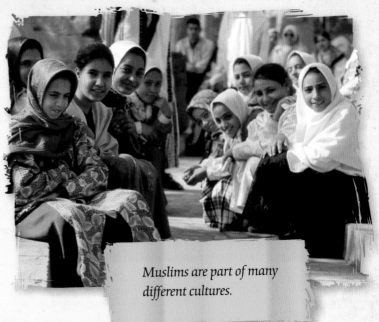

Muslims are part of many different cultures.

What do Muslims believe?

Muslims believe that there is one God, Allah. They believe that Allah is **eternal**, in other words, he was never born and he will never die. He has always been there. He is all-powerful and knows everything. He created the universe, the world and everything in it. He cares about what he made. He created human beings, and they have a duty to worship him, in return for all that he has done for them.

Muslims believe that the non-human natural world is Muslim, because it follows the laws that Allah laid down. However, Allah gave human beings free will – the freedom to choose right or wrong. This means that they are able to choose to be Muslim. Believing in Allah is not enough – they must live in the right way too. Muslims call this **niyyah** – intention. They believe that the intention to live a good life is vital to being a Muslim. This does not mean that they expect everyone to succeed all the time, but it is necessary to try as hard as they can. They believe that Allah is merciful and will judge what their intentions were.

Prophets

Muslims believe that human beings can only know about Allah because he has sent **prophets** to Earth. Some prophets are messengers, who bring a message from Allah in the form of scripture. Muslims believe that there have been 124,000 prophets, over thousands of years, and all of them were Muslims. The first prophet was Adam, the first man. The last prophet was a man called Muhammad. He was born in the country we now call Saudi Arabia in the year 570 CE. Muslims believe that Muhammad received messages from Allah, given to him by an angel. These messages were the words of Allah and can never be changed. They were collected together to form the Muslims' holy book, which is called the **Qur'an**.

The Shahadah

The most important beliefs of Islam are summed up in the **Shahadah**. This is also called the Declaration of Faith. In Arabic it is 'La ilaha illa-Llah, Muhamad rasulu-Allah'. This is usually translated as 'There is no God except Allah, and Muhammad is the messenger of Allah.' These are the first words said to a new-born Muslim baby, and the last words said by a Muslim who is dying, if they are still able to speak. Among observant Muslims, they are the first words said upon waking up, and the last words said before going to sleep. The Shahadah also forms part of the Call to Prayer (see page 23).

The Shahadah made into a picture.

Islam fact check

◆ Muslims believe that there is only one God. Muslims believe that Allah (the Arabic word for 'God') is the same God as that worshipped by Christians and Jews.

◆ The Muslim place of worship is called a **mosque** (masjid in Arabic).

◆ The Muslim holy book is called the Qur'an.

◆ The Muslim calendar dates from 622 CE. This is when Muhammad moved to Madinah, an event called the **hijrah**.

◆ The symbol most often used for Islam is a crescent moon and a star. No one really knows where this symbol came from, but many people believe it comes from the fact that Islam has its roots in desert countries. People travelled at night when it was cooler, and used the moon and stars to guide them, just as their religion guides them through life.

◆ There are estimated to be 1.3–1.5 billion Muslims in the world today, living in almost every country in the world. Scholars roughly estimate that there are around 3–6 million Muslims in the United States, about 1.5 million in Britain, and about 220,000 in Australia.

◆ In most of the countries in northern Africa and the Middle East, over half the population are Muslim. South Asia has the world's highest Muslim population, and Indonesia is the country with the most Muslims.

◆ In Europe, Islam is the second-largest religion after Christianity.

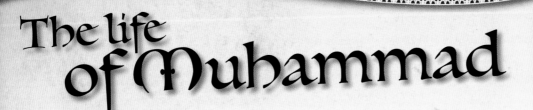

The life of Muhammad

You can find the places mentioned in this book on the map on page 44.

These traders today still live and work in similar ways to Muhammad.

Muhammad was born in the city of Makkah, in the country we now call Saudi Arabia. Muslims believe he was born in the year 570 CE, on the twelfth day of the third month. His mother, Amina, was a widow, because Muhammad's father had died before he was born. When Muhammad was six, his mother died and he was cared for by his grandfather. Two years later his grandfather died, and Muhammad's uncle began to look after him.

Makkah was an important trading centre, and Muhammad's uncle was a trader. From about the age of twelve, Muhammad began helping his uncle. By the time he was an adult, Muhammad had become well known for his honesty and goodness. He was given the nickname Al-Amin, which means 'the trustworthy one'. He began working for a wealthy woman called Khadijah, who was also a trader. When Muhammad was 25, he and Khadijah were married. Muhammad was respected, he was rich, he was happily married. It seemed that his life had everything he could possibly want.

However, Muhammad had always been a thoughtful man, and there were evidently times when he needed to be by himself. He needed to **meditate** about his life and the things that were happening in the world around him. He was unhappy about what he saw in the life of Makkah. There were wealthy people, but many of them spent their days gambling, drinking and fighting. The rich cheated the poor. The worship of **idols** was common, and often included **sacrifices**. Muhammad was sure that these things were wrong.

One night, when he was about 40 years old, Muhammad was meditating in a cave on Mount Hira. Muslims believe that he saw the angel Jibril (the Arabic version of Gabriel). Jibril was a messenger from Allah, giving Muhammad words of revelation that he must recite. Muslims believe that this was the first of the **revelations** of the Qur'an. As Muhammad stood up and walked out of the cave, he heard the angel say, 'Muhammad! You are Allah's messenger!'

Muhammad was terrified by this experience. He feared that he might be going mad, or that an evil force was trying to make him claim special powers for himself. He returned home and told Khadijah what had happened. She comforted him and went to talk to her cousin, an old man who was a devout Christian, and whose judgement she respected. He was sure that Muhammad had indeed seen a messenger from God. Khadijah became the first person to believe in the words that Muhammad spoke.

Some months later, Muhammad had another revelation. Then there was a gap of two years before the revelations began again. After this, Muhammad continued to receive messages and instructions from Allah for the rest of his life. For several years, Muhammad did not speak of his experiences except to his friends and family. Then the angel told him that he must go out and preach to the people of Makkah. His message was not well received. The people did not like being told that the way they lived was wrong. They made a lot of money from people coming to worship the idols, and they did not want to get rid of them in or

After several years, men from the neighbouring town of Yathrib heard Muhammad preaching. They were impressed and asked him to go to their town and become a religious leader there. At last Muhammad agreed. His journey to Yathrib (later called Madinah) is called the hijrah.

The Great Mosque in Makkah today, with Mount Hira in the background.

The Hadith

The most important teachings of Islam are those of the Qur'an, which Muslims believe were Allah's words, given to Muhammad by the angel Jibril. They also have enormous respect for the **Hadith**, which means 'traditions'. The Hadith are traditional teachings which go back to the time of Muhammad. There are two sorts of Hadith: the sacred and the prophetic. The sacred Hadith are so called because Muslims believe that they are teachings that came from Allah, although they were not part of the revelations of the Qur'an. The prophetic Hadith are teachings that were given by Muhammad himself, based on experiences in his life. They are valued very highly because Muslims respect Muhammad so much. Muslims today who are faced with a problem or difficulty and cannot find an answer in the Qur'an will look to the Hadith for guidance. This tells them what Muhammad said or did in the same or a similar situation.

The Mosque of the Prophet in Madinah today.

The hijrah

You can find the places mentioned in this book on the map on page 44.

Muhammad made the dangerous journey to Yathrib (Madinah) in 622 CE. Yathrib was about 320 km (200 miles) from Makkah. The journey was dangerous because some of the people in Makkah had been unhappy with Muhammad's teachings. They wanted to get rid of him, and in the desert it would be easy to ambush and kill him. There are several stories in the Muslim tradition about how Allah protected Muhammad on the journey. One says that he was hiding in a cave when his enemies came right to the entrance, but because a spider had built its web and a bird was nesting there, they did not search it.

When Muhammad arrived in Yathrib, he was treated as an honoured prophet, a messenger from God. Everyone wanted him to go and stay in their house. To avoid offending anyone, Muhammad said he would let his camel choose where he was going to live. The camel knelt down at a spot where dates were laid out to dry. Muhammad bought the land and built a house there. Later, in part of the same site, he built a place of worship, where Muslims could meet for prayer. The site is still preserved and respected by Muslims as being the first mosque in the world.

Muhammad became a religious leader and also the leader of the city. Many people listened to his preaching, and began to follow the new religion. It became so popular that the city became known as Madinat-al-nabi, which means 'the City of the Prophet'. Later, this name was shortened to Madinah, which is the name still used today. The journey to Madinah was called the hijrah, which means 'the migration'. Muslims recognized that this was a very important event, so they began to number the years after it. The years of the Muslim calendar are therefore followed by the letters AH – After the Hijrah.

These Shi'ah Muslims are taking part in the festival of Ashura.

Those who lead prayer and deliver sermons in mosques are called **imams**, but the title has a special meaning for Shi'ah Muslims. Shi'ahs believe that there were twelve imams (some Shi'ahs say seven) who were given special powers by Allah, just as Muhammad was. They believe that the first imam was Ali, whose power passed to his son, and so on. The last imam, called the Mahdi, did not die, but disappeared mysteriously in 880 CE. They believe that one day he will return, and bring about an age of justice and righteousness. Until he does, the teaching of the imams is in the hands of 'Doctors of the Law', called **Ayatollahs**. Ayatollah means 'sign of Allah'. In 1979, the Ayatollah Khomeini removed the leader of Iran from power and set up a religious state. Shi'ah Islam is now the state religion in Iran.

The festival of Ashura

In the month of Muharram every year, Shi'ah Muslims take part in a festival at Karbala, where the body of Husayn, one of Muhammad's grandsons, is buried. Husayn was killed in battle in 681 CE, fighting for the position of khalifah. Shi'ah Muslims remember this as a time when evil (the victorious Yazid) triumphed over good (the defeated Husayn). During the festival, people remember the dreadful deaths of Husayn and his family. There are daily gatherings where emotions are stirred up until most people are weeping and they all promise to live their lives to ensure that evil cannot triumph again. There are processions and plays showing the events of the battle and the martyrdoms. Sometimes men in the processions gash themselves with knives and beat themselves with chains, as a way of remembering what Husayn suffered.

The Qur'an

There are different versions of the story of the revelation to Muhammad. According to one version, the first revelation of the Qur'an came when Muhammad was meditating in a cave on Mount Hira, just outside Makkah. Muslims believe he saw an angel who came towards him, carrying a roll of silk on which words were written in fiery letters. The angel said, 'Iqra!' which means 'Recite!' Like many people in those days, Muhammad could not read or write, and he said that he could not read the words. The angel repeated the command three times, and each time Muhammad said that he could not do so. He said afterwards that he felt a pressure building up inside him, and something gripping his chest and his throat so tightly that he felt he was going to die. Then he found that he was able to repeat the words.

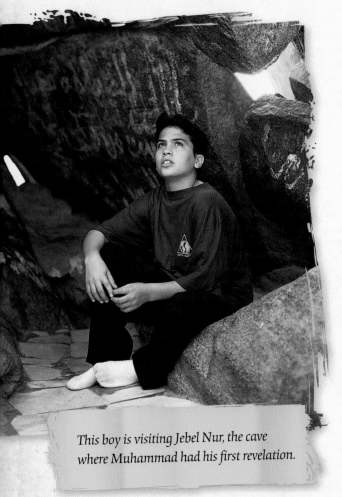

This boy is visiting Jebel Nur, the cave where Muhammad had his first revelation.

Recite!
In the name of your Lord,
Who created all humanity out of a single drop of blood!
Speak these words aloud!
Your Lord is the Most Generous One,
He who taught the use of the Pen, taught man that which he did not know.
(Surah 96:1–5)

The angel identified himself as Jibril, and told Muhammad that he was to be Allah's messenger. Some months later, Muhammad had another vision, when the angel appeared to him as a huge pair of eyes staring at him, and became an enormous figure whose feet touched the horizon. Whichever way he turned, Muhammad could still see the figure. Again, he was terrified.

For the rest of his life, Muhammad continued to receive messages from God. A few times, he saw the angel again. Most times, the messages came as voices in his head. There is a tradition that sometimes he could hear the voices perfectly, at other times they appeared muffled.

Muhammad's visions

Muslim tradition says that Muhammad always knew when the visions were going to happen, so he would lie down, usually wrapped in the cloak which he used as blanket. He sometimes appeared very hot, even in cold weather, and would sweat a great deal.

He often seemed to become unconscious. The visions always made him feel that he was close to death. When the visions came to an end, he would sit up, his normal self again, and repeat what he had been told. It was the duty of his friends as well as of Muhammad himself to memorize the words, so that nothing of the message was lost.

What Muslims believe about the Qur'an

Muslims believe that the Qur'an is made up of the direct words of Allah, given to human beings through Muhammad. Muslims respect the teachings which Muhammad gave himself, but they are in a different class from the words of the Qur'an, which came from Allah and can never be changed. This is why they believe that the actual words of the Qur'an are so important. However, there are different ways to understand its meaning. Some Muslims follow a literal interpretation of the Qur'an, while others see things in a more symbolic way.

Muslims do not believe that Muhammad was the first person to receive a revelation from Allah. However, they believe that the revelations given to other people (for example, the Torah of the Jews or the Gospels of the Christians) have been changed by the people who wrote them down and by subsequent generations. They can no longer be relied upon to perfectly represent the words of Allah.

This handwritten copy of the Qur'an is over 200 years old.

Translations

Arabic is the language of the Qur'an. It uses letters that are very different from the Roman letters used in English and most European languages. This means that an Arabic word needs to be transliterated (changed into another alphabet) as well as translated (giving its meaning). There are no exact equivalents to the sound of Arabic letters in the Roman alphabet. This means that the letters that give the sound nearest to the original have to be used. Opinions have changed about which letters should be used, and this is why many Arabic words have more than one spelling in the Roman alphabet. For example, Muhammad's name can be spelled Mohamed, Mohammad and Mahomet. Makkah is often spelled Mecca. The differences are not wrong, they are just alternatives. The spellings used in this book are the ones now thought to give the closest sound to the original word.

A beautifully decorated copy of the Qur'an, open at the first two surahs.

Surahs

The Qur'an is made up of chapters called surahs. There are 114 surahs altogether, which are of different lengths. The longest is surah 2, which has 286 verses. The shortest is surah 103, which has only three verses. Except for one (surah 9) the surahs all begin with the words 'In the name of Allah, the gracious, the merciful'. The surahs are not in the order that the words were received by Muhammad. Muslims believe that not long before he died, Muhammad received instructions about the order in which they were to be kept.

Muslims believe that the words of the Qur'an must be preserved exactly as they were given. Muhammad ensured that this happened by repeating all the revelations to his friends and family, who all learned them off by heart. In those days, not many people could read or write, and learning things like this was the usual way in which important words were remembered. Islamic tradition states that the complete Qur'an was written down within twenty years of Muhammad's death, and it has never been altered.

Hafiz

Muslims believe that the Qur'an is the most important book that has ever existed, because it contains the words of Allah. To help to ensure that it can never be changed in any way, and because they believe it is so important, many Muslims learn it completely by heart. Anyone who has done this is allowed to use the title **hafiz** as part of their name. They are very respected by other Muslims.

Translations

The Qur'an has been translated into over 40 other languages, but for worship it is only ever used in Arabic. This is because Muslims believe that the translations can never give the exact sense of Allah's words. Even Muslims who do not speak Arabic know some of the words of the Qur'an in the original language, and use it for worship.

What does the Qur'an say?

The surahs which Muhammad received first are about the one-ness of Allah, Muhammad's role as a prophet, and about what will happen at the Last Judgement. Later surahs are about everyday matters such as marriage and the law, and how to live as a Muslim. The surahs are labelled as Meccan or Medinan surahs, based on where they were received.

Decorations

There are never any pictures in a mosque. Muhammad said that they must not be used, because there was a danger that people might begin to worship them. (Muslims regard any pictures of Allah or holy beings as blasphemy, in other words insulting Allah.) Instead of pictures, the mosque is beautifully decorated. The carpets are often made in rich colours with patterns on them. Green is popular because it was Muhammad's favourite colour, and a rich turquoise blue is often used, too. The walls may have tiles or other paintings to make them beautiful. These may be pictures of flowers or plants, or geometric patterns. Marble pillars and dangling glass chandeliers are other ways in which a mosque can be made to look special.

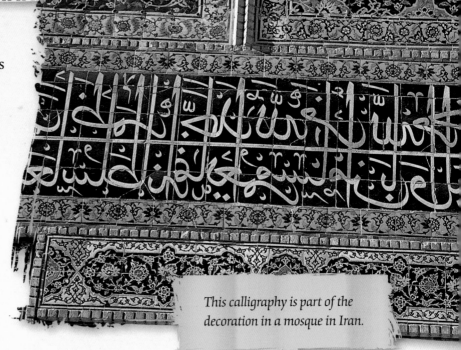

This calligraphy is part of the decoration in a mosque in Iran.

Calligraphy

A special form of decoration is Islamic **calligraphy**. Calligraphy is the art of beautiful handwriting, and especially the art of making writing into pictures. It began when people began to write out verses from the Qur'an. They wanted to make them as beautiful as possible, to show how much they valued them. At first, the words were written on paper or parchment, using sharpened reeds dipped in ink. Later, tiles and pottery began to be decorated in this way too. Pictures can be made using letters, phrases from the Qur'an, or prayers. In the mosque, these can help the people to worship.

Musa's view

Musa is 12, and lives with his family in London.

I go to the madrasah for **Islamiat** (the study of Islam) on Saturdays, and usually for a couple of hours after school, so that I can learn Arabic and the Qur'an. Sometimes if I've had a hard day at school, it feels like doing extra work, but it's totally different from the way we work at school. I know some of the Qur'an off by heart now, and the more I learn Arabic the easier it is to understand. The imam who teaches us really tries hard to make us understand, and I enjoy feeling that I'm learning more about something that's so important.

The Ka'bah

You can find the places mentioned in this book on the map on page 44.

The Ka'bah is the most important building in the world for Muslims. It is Islam's holiest **shrine**. It stands in the central courtyard of the Great Mosque, in the centre of Makkah. It was already very old when Muhammad was alive, and no one really knows where it came from. There are two traditions. One says that it was built by Adam, the first man, as the first place in the world to worship Allah. Then it was rebuilt by the prophet Ibrahim and his son Isma'il to thank Allah for saving Isma'il's life (see page 33). Ibrahim is the prophet whom Jews and Christians call Abraham. The other tradition says that it was built first by Ibraham and Isma'il. Both accounts agree that it was built to worship Allah.

At the time of Muhammad, the Ka'bah was a centre of worship, but worship of idols. It contained over 360 statues and altars, for worshipping many different gods. Many people came to worship these idols. This was one of the reasons why Makkah was an important centre of pilgrimage and such a rich city at the time of Muhammad. After Muhammad had converted the Makkans to Islam, all the idols were thrown out of the city, and the Ka'bah became a centre of worship for Allah. Ever since, it has been the shrine that all Muslims face when they pray.

The Ka'bah is built of brick, and is cube-shaped (ka'bah means 'cube'). It measures 15 metres (49 feet) long by 10 metres (33 feet) wide and 14 metres (46 feet) high. Inside it is a room whose walls are covered with quotations from the Qur'an. It is a rare and special privilege for a Muslim to be allowed to pray inside the Ka'bah. He can pray and – for the only time in his life – face alternately in all four directions as he prays.

During the time of the Hajj, the Ka'bah is covered with a black cloth beautifully decorated with the words of the Qur'an in gold embroidery. At the end of Hajj the cloth is cut into small pieces and pilgrims are able to take these home with them.

The Black Stone.

The Black Stone

In one corner of the Ka'bah is the Black Stone. This is an oval stone about 18 cm (7 inches) long which is probably a meteorite. Today it is set in silver. It was very old at the time of Muhammad and there are many stories about it. One story says that Adam found it in the desert, when it was gleaming white, but the sins of human beings have caused it to turn black. Another story says that angels took it to heaven for safe keeping at the time of the Great Flood, and returned it when Ibrahim and Isma'il rebuilt the Ka'bah.

The Mosque of the Prophet

The Mosque of the Prophet is in Madinah and was built over the place where Muhammad's body was buried. Muhammad's tomb lies beneath a green dome, and the mosque has been extended and enlarged several times since his death. The mosque also contains the graves of the khalifahs Abu Bakr and Umar. It is an important place of pilgrimage for Muslims, especially when they have been on Hajj to Makkah.

The Mosque of the Dome of the Rock

The Mosque of the Dome of the Rock is in Jerusalem. It was built in the seventh century CE and was restored in the sixteenth century. Jerusalem is the third holiest city for Muslims, after Makkah and Madinah. They believe that this mosque marks the place where Muhammad was taken to heaven on the Night of the Journey (see page 35). They also believe that the rock on which this mosque is built is the place where the call to judgement will be sounded on the Day of Judgement.

Inside the Mosque of the Dome of the Rock in Jerusalem.

Muhammad and the Black Stone

When Muhammad was a young man, the Ka'bah was being repaired, and the Black Stone had been removed. When it was due to be replaced, a squabble broke out among the different tribes in Makkah as to who should be given the honour of carrying it. Muhammad settled the quarrel by spreading a rug on the ground, and lifting the Black Stone onto it. The heads of the tribes then took a corner of the rug each, so that they could all carry it. Muslims say that it was because of incidents like these that Muhammad was so respected, even before he began to have revelations from Allah.

Hajj – pilgrimage to Makkah

Every Muslim who is healthy and who can afford it is expected to go on a pilgrimage to Makkah at least once in their life. To be a true Hajj, the pilgrimage must take place between 8 and 13 Dhul-Hijjah, the last month of the Muslim year. Every year, about two million pilgrims go to Makkah at this time. Pilgrimage at other times of the year is called **Umrah**, and is not considered so important.

Pilgrims on Hajj wear special clothes called ihram.

Ihram

Whilst they are on Hajj, pilgrims are expected to live in a special way called **ihram**. They should not swear or quarrel. Any sexual contact is forbidden, even if husbands and wives are travelling together. To show that the thoughts of all pilgrims are pure, women do not cover their faces, even if they normally do so. No one wears jewellery or cosmetics, or uses scented soap. Pilgrims do not cut their hair or trim their nails.

The special clothes for Hajj are also called ihram. Every man wears two white sheets without seams, one wrapped around the lower body, the other draped over the left shoulder. They do not cover their heads, though they may carry an umbrella as protection against the sun. Women wear a plain dress with long sleeves, leaving only their face and hands uncovered. All pilgrims go barefoot or in open sandals. Everyone dresses in the same way, so that there are no distinctions between rich and poor. Everyone is equal before Allah.

Performing Hajj

As soon as a pilgrim arrives in Makkah, they hurry to the Ka'bah, and circle it seven times. They walk quickly, running if possible. Those close enough touch or kiss the Black Stone. Those further away raise their hands towards it. Then they go to pray near Maqam Ibrahim (Ibrahim's place). They hurry seven times between two small hills not far from the Ka'bah. Today, the hills are linked by a broad corridor. This reminds pilgrims how Hajar, the handmaiden of Ibrahim's wife, ran between the two hills desperately looking for water for her son Isma'il. The well they believe Hajar found is called the Well of Zamzam, in the courtyard of the Great Mosque. Pilgrims drink from it and often collect some water to take home for friends and family.

You can find the places mentioned in this book on the map on page 44.

Wuquf

On 9 Dhul-Hijjah, the pilgrims travel to the Plain of Arafat, about 20 km (12 miles) from Makkah. Here they take part in the 'stand before Allah', called **wuquf**. This is the most important part of the pilgrimage. They stand from midday to sunset, thinking about Allah, and asking him to forgive all the wrong things they have done in their life. Muslims believe that if it is properly performed, wuquf means that all a person's sins are forgiven. The pilgrims return to Muzdalifah for the evening prayers and to camp overnight.

The plain of Arafat during Hajj.

On the morning of 10 Dhul-Hijjah, the pilgrims go to Mina, where there are three stone pillars. They throw stones at these, as a reminder of how Ibrahim drove away the devil who was tempting him. After the first pillar has been stoned, pilgrims sacrifice a sheep or a goat. This is part of the festival of Id-ul-Adha, in which Muslims all over the world take part. Male pilgrims then either cut their hair or shave their heads, and women cut off a lock of their hair. They do this because it is what Muhammad did. They take off their special pilgrim clothes and return to their normal clothes. They camp at Mina for three more days, and then travel back to Makkah for a last walk around the Ka'bah. They drink as much as they can from the Well of Zamzam, and then the Hajj is ended. Some pilgrims return home, others stay to visit other holy sites in the area.

Hussain's view

Hussain is 14 and lives in Lahore, Pakistan.
My uncle went on Hajj a couple of years ago. It's so popular now you have to apply for a place. The whole family helped him get ready, making sure he didn't forget anything. In a lot of families, I know people club together to get the money to send one person. We couldn't wait for him to come home and tell us all about it. I just can't imagine that many people all gathered together. He said that it's safer now than it used to be, but in the old days people sometimes used to be crushed to death in the crowd. He brought us a bottle of water from the Well of Zamzam. We looked at his ihram clothes, which he brought home so that when he dies he can be buried in them. He said the whole Hajj was a wonderful experience and not like anything else in the whole of his life. I really look forward to the day when I can go.

Celebrations

There are many festivals in the Islamic calendar. One of the most important is **Ramadan**, which is the ninth month of the Muslim calendar. Every year, for the 29 or 30 days of this month, Muslims fast during the hours of daylight. The instruction to perform the fast comes from the Qur'an, and the observance of it goes right back to the days of Muhammad.

All eating finishes before dawn, so the day starts well before this. To avoid confusion, lists are published in different places announcing the time when fasting must begin and end. Breakfast is usually a high-energy meal, to give a good start to the day. At sunset, there is a light snack, followed by a main meal later.

Giving thanks before breaking the fast during Ramadan.

Why do Muslims fast?

Muhammad taught his followers that the fasting is very important, because it is a sign that they have submitted to Allah. It shows that Allah is the most important thing in their life – far more important than food and drink. It is also a great 'leveller'. Fasting reminds the rich what hunger is like, and helps them remember to be compassionate to the poor.

The Muslim calendar

Islam follows a lunar year. This means that each new month begins on the night of the new moon. A month therefore lasts 29 or 30 days, so is slightly shorter than the 'Western' calendar months. This means that each year is about ten days shorter than a Western year. The months move back through the seasons, year by year, so that over several years each month will have occurred in every season. This is particularly important for celebrations like Ramadan, which involve fasting during daylight hours. Away from the equator, days vary in length throughout the year, so the time of fasting is a great deal longer in July than in January.